Living the L....

HARD
EASY

WORKBOOK

a get-real
workbook for
getting the life
you want

ARTHUR F. COOMBS III

EBook ISBN: 978-1-949165-33-3

Trade Paperback ISBN: 978-1-949165-32-6

Editorial work and production management by The Book Break

Edited by Suzanna Marie Collet and Kailey Urbaniak

Cover design adapted by Suzanna Marie Collet

Interior print and eBook design and layout by Kailey Urbaniak

Published by Scrivener Books

Scrivener Books EBook Edition 2021

Scrivener Books Trade Paperback Edition 2021

Printed in the USA

CONTENTS

INTRODUCTION

WHAT THE LAW OF HARD-EASY IS AND WHAT IT CAN DO FOR YOU

This workbook is a companion tool to help you get down to the nuts and bolts, dig deep, and apply the lessons from my book, *Hard Easy: A Get Real Guide for Getting What You Want.*

I first plunged into the concept of this law when a gritty, veteran cowboy gave some sage advice on the cattle drive: "Coombs, you can live Hard-Easy or Easy-Hard. It's your choice." Some days I can still hear the voice of Gordon from across the stream as BigDog (my horse) refuses to cross where I want him to. Those words changed my life. And I hope they change yours.

If you have not yet read *Hard Easy*, here are a few things you should know:

First, if you are looking to improve your life, *Hard Easy* and this workbook are for you. If you are looking for someone to coddle or absolve you of poor decisions, you will be disappointed—and my book is not for you.

These tools are for readers who want to better their lives and are not looking for a silver bullet, magic pill, or hot, trendy success secret that, like a fad diet, won't lead to lasting, positive change.

With that in mind, please do not instantly accept anything in this text as doctrine or absolute truth.

My ideas deserve your scrutiny. I want you to reason with your head and then listen with your heart. Because I know that when the heart is convinced that the head has it right, you are motivated to move.

- The law of Hard-Easy is simple: putting in the hard work first makes things easier down the road.

- The reverse is also true: choosing Easy first makes things harder down the road.

If you have already read *Hard Easy,* you will remember that the law of Hard-Easy...

- is sequential and causal.

- is an accumulation of small decisions over time.

- is directly related to our choices, not our circumstances.

- is a natural and universal law, just like gravity. It affects everyone equally, regardless of how much or how little they know about it.

One of the major concepts of the law of Hard-Easy is delayed gratification. At the end of each chapter, you'll find a short list of reflection activities. Answer the questions. These activities will help you gather your thoughts and formulate bigger plans. When you finish chapter 22, go back and review your answers. Use these reflections to define and create a plan of action for your first goal. If while completing these reflection activities you become eager to get started on your goal *now,* I urge you to delay that gratification. First, get all the information so you can make informed, strategic decisions.

Review and complete the activities in this workbook as often as necessary to set new goals and help you stay on the path of Hard-Easy.

With this knowledge, you will be able to make minute changes that will have massive benefits for your future self. Those changes will feel awkward and challenging at first—and you may not even see any discernible results. But I promise you that, over time, they will build momentum.

Once you are truly in control, you will feel a growing appreciation for the law and how it works. You will have an increase in confidence, poise, and tranquility.

1 THE PARABLE OF THE SUMMIT

LEARNING FROM THE WISDOM OF OTHERS

What is wisdom? And why should you listen to me about this Hard-Easy thing?

PRINCIPLE

Accumulating wisdom is good. Applying that wisdom to help yourself and others to make the best possible choices while avoiding pitfalls is ideal.

CHAPTER RECAP

In my parable of the summit in chapter one of *Hard Easy*, this principle is represented by my ability to see a nasty highway collision from my vantage point on top of Mount Timpanogos—a collision up ahead that my son driving up the interstate could not possibly have known about.

- Wisdom is the combination of knowledge plus experience.

- Wisdom typically develops with age.

- Listening to the wisdom of those you trust can be beneficial.

PAUSE AND THINK

- Are there times in your life when the wisdom of others helped you make a good choice—or avoid a poor choice? Reflect on one example.

_____

_____

_____

_____

_____

_____

_____

_____

_____

- Are there times in your life when you ignored the wisdom of others and later discovered you wished you had followed their advice? Give one example.

_____

_____

_____

_____

_____

_____

_____

_____

_____

_____

_____

_____

_____

_____

_____

_____

_____

_____

_____

_____

TAKEAWAY

Sometimes the course ahead looks like smooth sailing, but when you combine knowledge with experience—sometimes from another source you trust—you gain a different perspective.

2 WALMART AT 2:00 A.M. AND FINDING YOUR WHY

I 'm a big believer in communicating the why. I try to incorporate this principle in much of my writing. If people understand why they're doing something, they're much more likely to value the task and to give it their best. That's why I pulled my son out of bed at 2:00 a.m.

PRINCIPLE

We can't impose wisdom upon or force someone to make wise decisions. Likewise, wisdom cannot be imposed upon us. Although we might or might not listen to mentors whose advice can guide us, we always need to arrive at our own wisdom.

CHAPTER RECAP

My son Kai did not have a why to apply Hard-Easy to his schooling. He found his why when I brought him to Walmart at 2:00 am. He saw that he could do things easy now, but it would be hard for him later. The father-son wrestling match we used to have every day to get him to do his school work has stopped. I do not tell Kai when, where, and how to do his homework. He manages it himself.

- While you cannot impose wisdom on others, you can help them find their why.

- The concept of Hard-Easy is simple, but it's easy to ignore or take for granted.

PAUSE AND THINK

- In what areas of your life are you most resistant to living Hard-Easy? List a few examples that come to mind.

_____

_____

_____

_____

- What whys can you identify that encourage you to live Hard-Easy in spite of that resistance? Jot down some ideas.

- Are you more trusting of wisdom, or are you more like Kai and want to see things for yourself? Reflect honestly.

_____

_____

_____

_____

_____

_____

_____

_____

_____

_____

_____

_____

_____

_____

_____

_____

_____

_____

_____

_____

TAKEAWAY

We are far better at motivating ourselves, more than anyone else trying to encourage us. Self-management becomes easier when we know our why for living Hard-Easy.

3 NEANDERTHALS DON'T HAVE 401(K)S

THE GENETIC "HARD" WIRING OF THE INSTANT-GRATIFICATION-CRAVING, EASY-HARD BRAIN AND HOW TO BEAT IT

Our brains have evolved to seek instant gratification. Luckily, nature also added the prefrontal cortex.

PRINCIPLE

When we understand where the impulse for instant gratification comes from and how it operates in our lives, we are better able to overcome that impulse through practice.

CHAPTER RECAP

Getting what we want now doesn't necessarily get us to the core of what we really want. As we learn from lottery winners in chapter 3, there tends to be a direct correlation between how difficult something is to obtain and how much we value it.

We see in the gift-card study from this chapter that impulsive behavior is not the only way to get your brain to release dopamine. You can get a sense of euphoria—although not quite to the same intensity—when you delay gratification (living Hard-Easy). People who don't practice restraint jeopardize a future they can't even conceive is possible.

But impulse control doesn't happen automatically. It's like a muscle—the more you exercise it, the stronger the prefrontal cortex's ability to control your impulses becomes.

- Our brains are genetically hardwired for instant gratification.

- We have the ability to resist impulses and delay gratification.

- You can make a habit of Easy-Hard or Hard-Easy. Both yield euphoria.

- The more you practice resisting instant gratification, the easier it becomes.

- Embrace the boredom of Hard and find the excellence of Easy.

PAUSE AND THINK

- When we procrastinate, we're usually seeking instant gratification by putting off the hard task. What kinds of things do you tend to procrastinate? Make a list, starting with areas such as relationships, spirituality, education, career, retirement, and travel.

_____

_____

_____

_____

_____

_____

_____

_____

_____

_____

_____

_____

_____

- From your procrastination list, pick out the trends that will yield the future results you most want to avoid. List them here.

_____

_____

_____

_____

_____

_____

_____

_____

_____

_____

_____

_____

_____

_____

_____

_____

_____

_____

_____

_____

_____

_____

- Now, narrow your list to two or three ways you tend toward Easy-Hard. Keep this list close at hand.

_____

_____

_____

_____

_____

_____

_____

_____

_____

_____

_____

_____

_____

_____

_____

_____

TAKEAWAY

If you seek greatness, you have to commit yourself to mastery, and that can be hard. If you are dabbling, you are not fully committed. Perfecting a skill is hard and sometimes boring. Push through the boredom and find Easy in excellence.

4 SEDUCED BY EASY

HOW EASY TRICKS YOU AND HOW YOU CAN FIGHT BACK

E asy is a boldfaced, seductive, dirty liar. It takes your fears and uses them against you, and it's a master marketer, making a pitch that sounds amazingly good to our Neanderthal brain.

But you can fight back.

PRINCIPLE

Choosing to live Hard-Easy doesn't immunize us from failure and disappointment. But when we live Hard-Easy, we see failure not as an impenetrable wall but as a stepping-stone to ultimate success.

CHAPTER RECAP

In chapter 4, I talk about the fix—the endorphin rush after the long run, the view from the summit after climbing a mountain, either literal or figurative.

When Easy sings its siren song at the foot of the mountain, remember, Thomas Edison made more than ten thousand prototypes before he hit on the right combination of materials and processes to create an efficient light bulb. Imagine if he had chosen the seductive Easy-Hard path at prototype #2—or prototype #9,999 for that matter?

Think of disappointment, discouragement, and doubt as a pack of velociraptors. They all hunt together to bring you down on behalf of their master, Easy-Hard. But you can get these snarling razor-toothed predators to transform into elation, courage, and belief—creatures that serve you instead of hunt you by using a phrase that hardens your resolve and sharpens your focus: "Bring it, Hard!"

It's a rallying cry. Sports teams have their versions. Militaries have theirs. But "Bring it, Hard!" is mine. In chapter 4, I share example after example of people who apply similar mantras and choose not to let the bad circumstances of life steal another minute from them. They avoid victim mentality and complacency.

Keep in mind that giving yourself time to heal, grieve, mourn, rage, and crumple is not being a victim. It's part of the process. Meanwhile, complacency is the carbon monoxide of the soul—odorless, tasteless, and invisible—a mindset that permeates your life and suffocates your ambition.

If your complacency detector is beeping, take notice. If you've fallen into the complacency trap, listen to me: you are worth the extra effort.

When doubts creep in, and failure strikes a blow, do not retreat or quit. Reject victim mentality, stare complacency down and say, "Bring it, Hard!"

- Easy is a liar.

- Focus on the fix.

- "Many of life's failures are people who did not realize how close they were to success when they gave up." (Thomas Edison)

- Make "Bring it, Hard!" your mantra as you charge toward the obstacles that will make you stronger.

- The victim mentality—no matter how justified—is self-sabotage.

- Don't hit snooze on the complacency alarm.

PAUSE AND THINK

- What is your fix? What reward motivates you to press forward? Pick something that feels powerful.

_____

_____

_____

_____

_____

_____

_____

_____

_____

_____

_____

_____

_____

- What does success mean to you? What does it look like? Close your eyes and imagine it. Now write it.

_____

_____

_____

_____

_____

_____

_____

_____

_____

_____

_____

_____

_____

_____

_____

_____

_____

_____

_____

_____

_____

_____

_____

- Where are you confronted with disappointment, discouragement, and/or doubt? What other velociraptors are trying to hurt you? Be specific.

_____

_____

_____

_____

_____

_____

_____

_____

_____

_____

_____

_____

_____

_____

_____

_____

_____

_____

_____

_____

_____

- Where do you see complacency in your life? What is the root of it? Write down the first response that comes to mind. You can always come back and change your answer.

_____

_____

_____

_____

_____

_____

_____

_____

_____

_____

_____

_____

_____

_____

_____

_____

_____

_____

_____

- Pick one velociraptor out of your pack. Identify and write down one thing you can do to look it in the face and say, "Bring it, Hard!"

_____

_____

_____

_____

_____

_____

_____

_____

_____

_____

_____

_____

_____

_____

_____

_____

_____

_____

_____

_____

_____

TAKEAWAY

The Hard-Easy path looks unpleasant. Swamps. Quicksand. Terrifyingly steep cliffs.

Hailstorms and darkness.

And the Easy-Hard path beckons with its gentle, nondisruptive trail into a sunshine-filled meadow.

But the paths go on beyond the horizon. The Easy-Hard path that started so pleasantly leads to a hard, frightening place that's oppressive, dark, unfulfilling, frustrating, and painful, while the Hard-Easy path takes you to a glorious vista surrounded by blue skies.

I desperately want you to summon your inner warrior and shout, "Bring it, Hard!" to your life. Utter those magic words, even if you don't quite have faith in them yet.

5 A BRIEF WARNING ABOUT CRISIS HIGHS

E ven if you are pumped up about living Hard-Easy now and want to sprint down that hard path, it's best to take the time to build a plan.

PRINCIPLE

Whenever possible, it's best we think before we act. Otherwise, we run the risk of being in constant crisis mode.

CHAPTER RECAP

In this chapter, we reflect on reacting on impulse. Even in the name of making a change for the good, reacting on impulse can cause more harm than good. Those who live Easy-Hard are often reactionary in everyday scenarios—impulsively responding to problems, people, situations, or challenges without forethought, allowing the moment to drive them. Right or wrong, they act in the heat of the moment. And most of the time, it turns out to be wrong.

Living in crisis can actually be addictive. If you're feeling the need to kamikaze into kicking complacency's ass, step back for a minute from this knee-jerk reaction so you don't sabotage yourself. Don't feed the chaos.

- Beware of the crisis high.

- Think before you act whenever possible.

PAUSE AND THINK

- How often are you in crisis mode? Answer honestly.

_____

_____

_____

_____

_____
_____
_____
_____
_____
_____
_____
_____
_____
_____
_____

- Think of a time when you acted impulsively in the heat of the moment. It's probably embarrassing or even painful to recall. In retrospect, how would you have acted differently if you'd taken the time to think before acting? Describe.

_____
_____
_____
_____
_____
_____
_____
_____

_____

_____

_____

_____

_____

_____

_____

_____

_____

_____

_____

_____

_____

_____

_____

_____

_____

- First, think of the last big decision you made (use whatever criteria you feel appropriate to define "big decision"). How much thought did you put into it before making it? Do you feel that this was enough? Why or why not?

_____
_____
_____
_____
_____
_____
_____
_____
_____
_____
_____
_____
_____
_____
_____
_____
_____
_____

TAKEAWAY

Don't act before you think. In fact, finish this book before you begin razing the Easy-Hard tendencies in your life.

6 THE CASE OF THE INTELLIGENT IDIOT AND THE VALUE OF A WISDOM LENS

Neither your intelligence nor the number of diplomas you have automatically helps you make the Hard-Easy choice. Even when we know better, we don't always make the wisest choices. Other times, two Hard-Easy choices conflict, and we must sacrifice one at the expense of the other. We can learn to recognize these situations and make the best decisions we can in order to keep moving forward on our Hard-Easy journey.

PRINCIPLE

Making the best decisions requires considering the best information possible. The ability to apply knowledge for your benefit and to achieve the best possible outcome— that's wisdom.

CHAPTER RECAP

In chapter 6, I introduce the stupidity score. This scoring metric of mine states, "The better we know, the dumber our stupid actions are." For this metric, we can rate the stupidity of an action on a scale of one to ten and our knowledge about that action on a separate scale of one to ten. Then we can check the gap between the two scores.

Ideally, they should match up—our actions should align with our knowledge. On the other hand, if our actions don't align with our knowledge, we risk becoming the intelligent idiot.

As with *Mike's Dilemma* and *The Chore Conundrum* examples in this chapter, sometimes we are presented with two Hard-Easy choices that conflict. You can use your expanded knowledge—or wisdom lens—from academics, experience, or both to judge which choice best aligns with the most beneficial outcome.

- Apply the wisdom lens to decisions so you don't end up becoming the intelligent idiot.

- Apply the wisdom lens when prioritizing one Hard-Easy path over another.

PAUSE AND THINK

- In what areas would you consider yourself an intelligent idiot—where do you have a high stupidity score? List as few or as many examples as you like.

_____

_____

_____

_____

_____

_____

_____

_____

_____

_____

_____

_____

_____

_____

_____

_____

_____

_____

_____

_____

_____

- Can you identify a time when two Hard-Easy paths collided? How did you decide which one to prioritize? Describe.

_____

_____

_____

_____

_____

_____

_____

_____

_____

_____

_____

_____

_____

_____

_____

_____

_____

_____

_____

TAKEAWAY

When you think about the areas in your life over which you need to exert control, you need an honest evaluation around Hard-Easy versus Easy-Hard. To get what you really want out of life, you need to examine your Hard-Easy options to ensure a larger payoff down the line. Only then can you become who you truly want to be.

7 LESSONS IN PHYSICS AND NATURAL LAWS

FLYWHEELS, COMPOUND INTEREST, AND MICRODECISIONS

What does it take to change?

Put another way, how long do you have to live the hard part of Hard-Easy before the easy part kicks in?

PRINCIPLE

Little efforts count, and it all comes down to our choices—all of them.

CHAPTER RECAP

In this chapter, we examine three concepts: the flywheel effect, compound interest, and the accumulation of microdecisions. We look at two examples of how no effort goes unrewarded, then apply that concept to living Hard-Easy.

As you consider the ways you get your flywheel moving, don't fall into the trap of believing that only big efforts count. Your flywheel's momentum will respond to small pushes and large pushes. It works the same way with decisions. Your microdecisions count.

This is the essence of the law of Hard-Easy. Every decision is an opportunity to increase the flywheel's momentum or to build and reinvest interest. In that light, there are no unimportant decisions. One seemingly small decision can alter your trajectory.

- How do I change? Some of the laws and mechanisms that govern Hard-Easy/Easy-Hard—and govern how you can change—are the flywheel effect, compound interest, and microdecisions.

- The flywheel effect: Every Hard action you take in your life is a push on your personal flywheel. Each push builds a momentum that will one day lead to Easy results.

- Compound interest: Hard-Easy living is

taking the interest in your actions and reinvesting that interest in a goal so the effort compounds over time, growing more rapidly as time goes on and compounding continues.

- **Microdecisions matter.**

PAUSE AND THINK

- Spend a day or two being mindfully aware of all the decisions you make—especially those you may overlook as decisions because you make them while on autopilot. Keep these pages with you to record the microdecisions you notice.

_____

_____

_____

_____

_____

_____

_____

_____

_____

- Analyze some of the decisions you would normally categorize as minor or unimportant. List 2-5 here. How can these decisions contribute to your flywheel's momentum?

_____

_____

_____

_____

_____

_____

_____

_____

_____

_____

_____

_____

_____

_____

_____

_____

_____

_____

_____

_____

_____

_____

_____

_____

_____

_____

_____

_____

_____

_____

_____

_____

_____

_____

TAKEAWAY

We never have a guarantee of immediate results. But when we step back at some future point and look at our efforts from a broad perspective, we can see that Hard did turn into Easy and that keeping Easy going is—dare I say it—easy.

8 HIGH-PROFILE CASE EXAMPLES OF EASY CRASHING INTO HARD

W e've reviewed several aspects of Hard-Easy versus Easy-Hard. What happens when we put them together in real-world examples?

PRINCIPLE

To reverse Easy, it must be met with an equal and opposite Hard.

CHAPTER RECAP

Consider what we learned from the examples of Enron, Watergate, Tiger Woods, and the manager of a convenience store. In each scenario, the number of microdecisions required to change trajectory and start pushing the flywheel again would have been minimal on day one of the Easy-Hard journey. As time went on, the amount of energy needed to reverse course and go back to Hard-Easy would have been immense.

Eventually, turning back became impossible.

- Sometimes the Hard of Easy-Hard erupts and your life and the lives of others can suddenly implode.

- Altering your trajectory is easy until it is hard.

- Popularity comes with Easy, while Hard is often shouldered individually.

- Find your passion and funnel it into the Hard-Easy current—and let it amplify your return.

- Get your actions flowing in the right direction in as many facets of your life as possible.

PAUSE AND THINK

- What other examples can you think of

(real or fictional) where it comes to
living Hard-Easy or Easy-Hard?

_____

_____

_____

_____

_____

_____

_____

_____

_____

_____

_____

_____

_____

_____

_____

_____

_____

_____

_____

_____

_____

_____

- Have you ever reversed the flywheel in your life?

_____

_____

_____

_____

_____

_____

_____

_____

_____

_____

_____

_____

_____

_____

_____

_____

_____

_____

_____

_____

_____

_____

_____

- What is a passion you could funnel into the Hard-Easy current to amplify your return? Choose something that excites you more than chilled, thin mint cookies.

_____

_____

_____

_____

_____

_____

_____

_____

_____

_____

_____

_____

_____

_____

_____

_____

_____

_____

_____

_____

TAKEAWAY

We're always in flux. The more we can get our actions flowing in the right direction in as many facets of our lives as possible, the greater our return when the Easy blossoms from the Hard.

9 IN PRAISE OF GRITS

One of the most challenging parts of living Hard-Easy is sticking with it throughout the struggle and despite the stumbling. How do we remain committed to the Hard path when we inevitably experience failure and disappointment along the way?

PRINCIPLE

Grit can only be forged in the hard phase of Hard-Easy. Despite difficult circumstances, we can always choose how we react to those circumstances. And To build muscle, we must first break it down.

CHAPTER RECAP

Dr. Angela Duckworth describes grit as "having stamina and sticking with your future, day in and day out . . . for years—and working really hard to make that future a reality."[1] A fixed mindset says, "I can't do this." A growth mindset—someone with grit—says, "I can't do this *yet.*"

But what about challenges that seem unreasonable?

Neurologist and psychiatrist Viktor Frankl—author of *Man's Search for Meaning*—observed from his experience as a Jewish prisoner in concentration camps that, "One could make a victory of those experiences, turning life into an inner triumph, or one could ignore the challenge and simply vegetate, as did a majority of the prisoners."[2]

Challenges are given equally to optimists and pessimists. Optimists are propelled by joy, faith, and the belief in yes. Pessimists are paralyzed by fear, doubt, and the belief in no.

Grit, a growth mindset, delayed gratification, and the ability and willpower to determine how you will react when faced with difficult circumstances are key traits to living Hard-Easy.

- Be one of the grits.

- Natural talent, genetics, wealth, intelligence, and social status do not matter as much as we think they do; what matters is the belief that you can develop abilities, no matter how much or little you have, through dedication and hard work.

- We have the freedom—even when all other freedoms are taken—to choose how we react to the situation we're in, no matter how dire it seems.

PAUSE AND THINK

- What is the end goal you desire? Go with your gut instinct. Be specific.

_____

_____

_____

_____

_____

_____

_____

_____

_____

_____
_____
_____
_____
_____
_____
_____
_____
_____
_____
_____
_____
_____
_____

- What are some failures or problems you may run into along the way? Be specific.

_____
_____
_____
_____
_____
_____
_____
_____
_____

_____
_____
_____
_____
_____
_____
_____
_____
_____
_____
_____
_____
_____
_____

- How can the concepts of grit, growth mindset, and delayed gratification help you achieve that goal despite the challenges you face? List 1-3 challenges and at least one way you can apply grit to each. Then list the possible results.

_____
_____
_____
_____
_____
_____

_____

_____

_____

_____

_____

_____

_____

_____

_____

_____

_____

_____

_____

_____

TAKEAWAY

When we find meaning in challenging circumstances and focus on the result, we accrue grit.
Seeking opportunity within challenge and finding
inner triumph in spite of all the pain and difficul-
ties surrounding you—that's Hard-Easy.

10 "I CAN'T BECAUSE . . ."
THE TOP EXCUSES OF ALL TIME

Excuses are constant traps along our journey. While grit, a growth mindset, and delayed gratification are reliable defenses against excuses, we must know our enemy in order to use those defenses most effectively.

PRINCIPLE

Excuses do not change results.

CHAPTER RECAP

Making excuses is a common, self-deceptive, Easy-Hard tactic. It's easy to make excuses for our shortcomings and mistakes. It's hard to confront our weaknesses, confess our misdeeds, and commence the difficult work of change. You need to recognize your favorite excuses and knock them out of your brain and vocabulary.

Here are the the top excuses discussed in chapter 10:

1. I want to change, but I can't.

2. I am only human.

3. Nature versus Nurture excuses.

4. I don't have the time or money to change.

5. I am not ready to change.

6. I don't know how to change.

7. What if I fail?

8. It's not going to work because nothing ever works out for me.

9. I don't want to change / I don't need to change.

10. I am too old / too young to change.

11. I'll change tomorrow.

Key Concepts

- Keep an eye out for these excuses in your life—if you see them, shoot them on sight.

- By being aware of the most common excuse patterns our brains throw at us, we can inoculate ourselves, putting ourselves on high alert for when we try to let ourselves off the hook and go Easy-Hard.

- There's no excuse for excuses.

PAUSE AND THINK

- What is step one for your goal? Write it down.

_____

_____

_____

_____

_____

_____

_____

_____

_____

_____

_____

_____

_____

- Which excuses are most tempting when you think of step one? Be honest.

_____

_____

_____

_____

_____

_____

_____

_____

_____

_____

- How can you defeat them? Brainstorm your ideas here.

_____

_____

_____

_____

_____

_____

_____

_____

_____

_____

TAKEAWAY

The principle of Hard-Easy teaches us that the more we practice taking ownership of our mistakes, the easier it becomes. When we try to deny and hide our weaknesses, mistakes, and limitations with excuses, they become more firmly rooted in our character. And the more ingrained they become, the faster our so-called character deteriorates.

Owning and correcting our bad or mediocre behavior while balancing on the fine line of not being too critical of ourselves shows deep integrity.

11 A FEW PRACTICAL WAYS TO HELP YOU IDENTIFY AND PURGE EXCUSES

You're at war with excuses. What kind of weapons do you have in your arsenal to help eradicate the enemy?

PRINCIPLE

Excuses are sedatives that only mask discomfort.

CHAPTER RECAP

In chapter 11, we look at a few methods for changing your brain from excuse mode to excel mode.

First, be aware that you are guilty of making excuses. Being aware puts you in a position to do something about it. Second, start keeping an excuse tracker: a spreadsheet, a little notebook, your phone—whatever. Begin with one excuse you catch yourself making and count how many times you use it over the course of two weeks. In your excuse tracker, write down the situation that sparked the excuse and start to identify triggers.

As you identify the excuse—or excuses—you may feel the impulse to criticize yourself.

Don't.

Exorcise shame. Shame leads to more excuses in a flawed effort to boost your self-esteem, but those excuses act only as a sedative.

Think-shift. Evolve from making excuses and justifications to generating solutions.

While you fortify yourself against excuse-making, find a flock of fellow achievers who invigorate you and encourage self-improvement. Don't seek approval from the masses.

- Use these tools to spot and stop excuses: being aware, using the tool tracker, identifying triggers, exorcising shame, and engaging in think-shift.

- Find your flock.

- Don't listen to those who subtly or not so subtly divert you from your dreams.

- Start.

PAUSE AND THINK

- Have any of your friends ever called you out on something? How did you react? Were they right? Did it lead to a course correction? Record your honest reflection.

_____

_____

_____

_____

_____

_____

_____

_____

_____

_____

_____

_____

_____

_____

_____

_____

_____

_____

_____

_____

_____

_____

_____

_____

_____

_____

_____

_____

- Take a moment right now to start your excuse tracker. As you think about the excuses cataloged in this chapter and other excuses, name a couple you think you use quite often. Jot them down and be on the lookout for them.

_____

_____

_____

_____

_____

_____

TAKEAWAY

Stop excuses and start.

Start with one yes.
Start with one no.
Start with one small act of kindness.
Start with one sit-up.
Start with cleaning one room.
Start with one "I am sorry. I was wrong."
Start with one payment toward a debt.
Start with one contact deleted.
Start with one written note of gratitude.
Start with one "I love you."

12 SILENCING THE TOXIC WHISPERS OF SHAME

"Shame corrodes the very part of us that believes we are capable of change," said Dr. Brené Brown.[1]

PRINCIPLE

A positive self-image fortifies willpower.

CHAPTER RECAP

I will never forget the dread that filled my heart when I was caught chewing gum in fourth grade. Those ten minutes with my nose to the chalkboard were the longest of my life.

Shame may work as a deterrent to keep others in line, but as a motivational tool, it sucks. Negative reinforcement is always counterproductive to positive behavioral change. These feelings of inadequacy undermine your ability to make good

choices and your power to leverage the prefrontal cortex, driving you to unhealthy coping strategies.

Learn the difference between shame and healthy guilt. (Shame = I am bad. Guilt = what I did was bad.)

Don't be the troll (what you may think is clever or inspired discipline or advice might just be shaming in disguise.)

Avoid the breeding grounds of comparison. Every moment spent being jealous is a moment wasted.

- Shame is a corrosive, destructive force that erodes our ability to choose Hard-Easy.

- While we may feel shame for our own shortcomings, we can also be the purveyors of shame.

- Don't give in to the temptation to compare yourself to others.

- **The best weapon we can use to fight shame is empathy.**

- Please don't chew gum around me.

  Okay, I take it back. Go ahead and chew gum around me. I need to take responsibility for my own internalized damage, be more self-aware, and not shift the responsibility to those around me for the negative emotions I feel when I hear gum being chewed. I myself am fighting to overcome the victim mentality.

PAUSE AND THINK

- Be on the lookout for shaming behaviors in yourself and in others. Learning to recognize it is necessary to avoid being someone who perpetuates it. Without judgement, write down shaming behaviors you notice from yourself or others over the course of a day or week.

_____

_____

- Who do you most often compare yourself to? What steps can you take to limit these comparisons? Can you hide their social media posts for a while? Write down some ideas and apply one of these steps for at least a week.

_____

_____

_____

_____

_____

_____

_____

_____

_____

_____

_____

_____

_____

_____

_____

_____

_____

_____

_____

- Actively seek to build empathy. When you find yourself tempted to judge or shame another, genuinely try to see things from their perspective. This will likely involve being uncomfortable, but discomfort is often necessary for growth. Tally the number of times you tried this exercise in a day or week and give an example.

TAKEAWAY

Shame creates such strong feelings of inadequacy that it prevents you from moving forward. Self-forgiveness—not judgment, shame, or self-criticism—strengthens your willpower and the ability to leverage Hard-Easy in your life.

13 INVASION OF THE BRAIN SNATCHERS

HOW THE QUEST FOR INSTANT GRATIFICATION ROBS US OF FREE WILL AND TRUE JOY

So far, we've reviewed the basics of both instant and delayed gratification. It's time to take a closer look.

PRINCIPLE

Delayed gratification is deeper gratification, and grit is far better to rely on than talent.

CHAPTER RECAP

In chapter 13, I share two personal experiences—the stories of the peach trees and my friend Steve—about what the fruits of delayed gratification look like (literally!) and what the fruits of a lifetime of instant gratification look like.

My little peach orchard testifies to the law of Hard-Easy, teaching us how sometimes it takes years for the Easy phase of Hard-Easy to manifest after devotion to Hard. But when it does, how sweet it is.

My friend Steve didn't have a vision of where he wanted to go. He had no why. Time after time, he chose the Easy path of instant gratification. And over the years, he began to harvest the Hard that follows in Easy-Hard.

In this chapter, I also look at how technology has, over decades, fed and worsened our Neanderthal addiction for instant gratification and subverted our ability to let our brains do their best work.

Researchers at the University of Albany found that, in addition to social media being potentially addictive (especially applications like Facebook and Instagram), the very act of using social media may condition the brain to be at greater risk for impulse-control problems. Beware the brain snatchers!

- Delayed gratification is deeper gratification.

- Each time you choose Hard-Easy over Easy-Hard, it moves your sustained efforts toward critical mass, where they will begin to produce fruitful results with less and less effort.

- Sometimes raw talent can be a negative; those who have the combination of a little talent and a gritty work ethic can surpass those who have tremendous raw talent but a lazy work ethic.

- Choosing Easy-Hard can reprogram the brain—which is part of the reason why Hard is hard.

PAUSE AND THINK

Keep your chosen goal in mind. Answer these questions honestly and specifically.

- What delayed-gratification reward are you working toward?

_____

_____

_____

_____

_____

_____

_____

_____

_____

_____

_____

_____

- What instant-gratification temptations do you face?

_____

_____

_____

_____

_____

_____

_____

_____

_____

_____

_____

_____

_____

_____

- What talents do you have that can help you achieve your goal?

_____

_____

_____

_____

_____

_____

_____

_____

_____

_____

_____

- What hard work can supplement that talent?

_____

_____

_____

_____

_____

_____

_____

_____

_____

_____

_____

_____

_____

_____

_____

_____

_____

_____

_____

Examine your relationship with social media. Answer these questions honestly and specifically.

- In what ways is your relationship healthy? Unhealthy?

_____

_____

_____

_____

_____

_____

_____

_____

_____

_____

_____

_____

_____

_____

_____

_____

- What are two small changes you could make to improve it?

_____

_____

_____

_____

_____

_____

_____

_____

TAKEAWAY

As you face Easy-Hard or Hard-Easy decisions every day, before you choose, remember me sitting beneath my peach trees eating my succulent, sweet peaches. And think of my friend Steve, who moves from job to job in a lonely existence because he didn't nurture his talent with hard work. Think for a moment how the decision you are about to make has the power to reprogram your brain.

Then make the Hard-Easy decision.

14 GARLIC AGAINST THE INSTANT-GRATIFICATION VAMPIRE

DEFENSES FOR WHEN INSTANT GRATIFICATION TRIES TO SUCK YOUR ATTENTION AWAY FROM HARD-EASY

Modern distractions combine with our naturally short attention spans to encourage multitasking. When we attempt to multitask, we're giving in to the temptation of instant gratification. Narrowing our focus to one task at a time is delayed gratification and yields bigger rewards.

PRINCIPLE

The depth of your focus directly correlates to your ability to make Hard-Easy decisions and withstand the tsunamis of instant gratification. It is in deep thought that we plant and grow our big dreams. If you do not think it, you cannot dream it. If you do not dream it, you cannot act on it and make it your reality.

CHAPTER RECAP

Focus is key. It sounds simple, but when it comes to fending off the vampire of instant gratification, focus is your wooden stake. To achieve deep focus, we need to give our minds the uninterrupted time to attain deeper, sustained, probing thoughts. When you think deeply, you have the ability to be more proactive as opposed to reactive.

What sucks is that while we are capable of infinite, boundless thought, most of us now have a shorter attention span than a goldfish.

In 2015, Microsoft commissioned a study on attention span. What did they find? The more you use social media and devour digital content, the more your ability to maintain longstanding focus erodes. Severely.[1]

Additionally, multitasking is a seductive, destructive myth. Not only is it scientifically impossible, but according to the research, attempts to multitask reduce productivity, increase mistakes, reduce your ability to sort relevant information from irrelevant details, and may even reduce memory function.[2]

When you cannot sustain deep thought during challenges, your ability to live Hard-Easy is drastically impeded. Thankfully, research suggests the damage doesn't have to be permanent.[3]

Try this. Pick a subject that has been perplexing you. Phoneless, find someplace you will not be interrupted. Think exclusively about your perplexing thought for a solid five minutes.

Then do it again tomorrow.

As with any new skill, you can build up your time, focus, and depth of thought. Don't sabotage yourself by thinking or pushing too hard, too fast.

What if you sustained this focused, deep thinking and combined it with deliberate actions, stubborn tenacity, and grit?

- Focus is key.

- The depth of your focus correlates with your ability to make Hard-Easy decisions, day in and day out.

- Your thoughts are the DNA of your character and your reality—so don't have the thought DNA of a goldfish.

- The ability to think deep can be difficult, but just like the flywheel effect, once it starts turning and momentum takes over, Hard shifts to Easy.

PAUSE AND THINK

- With your big goal in mind, decide on an amount of time you can dedicate to deep focus. It might be daily or a few times each week. Write down your scheduled time, and stick to it.

_____

_____

_____

_____

- Spend the next day or two looking specifically at the times you're tempted to multitask. Whether or not you choose to follow that temptation, make note of the results you get.

_____

_____

_____

_____

_____

_____

_____

_____

_____

_____

_____

_____

_____

_____

_____

TAKEAWAY

What if you could evaluate the outcomes of different life paths, see into the future, and make choices that would enable you to achieve your wildest dreams?

It starts with training yourself to move past the distractions, extending your attention span beyond that of a goldfish, and immersing yourself in an environment that lets you plunge your mind into deep, deep thought.

Only then will you be armed with the deep focus—the garlic that repels the distracting vampire of instant gratification—to consistently achieve and overcome on the path of Hard-Easy.

15 YOU NEED A PURPOSE, A PLAN, AND A VISION

IN OTHER WORDS, YOU NEED TO BECOME A SALMON PERSON

Purpose can be a tough idea to get a handle on because it isn't as concrete or measurable as our goals. However, having an identifiable purpose is a significant indicator of whether a person will finish the journey and achieve the goal. Purpose keeps us going.

So, what is purpose, and how can you define yours?

PRINCIPLE

Purpose gives life meaning and direction and fosters hope for the future. Expanding our purpose beyond ourselves to help others is the surest path to happiness.

CHAPTER RECAP

Living Hard-Easy demands that you have a purpose in life. Purpose acts as both the anchor that keeps you grounded and the guiding star that inspires you to continue moving forward.

Idaho salmon will travel nine hundred miles upstream—while climbing seven thousand feet!—before they finally reach their destination.

Those with purpose—the ones who live Hard-Easy—are positive, upbeat, and enthusiastic. They spend their lives swimming upstream to reach their goals. They find ways to overcome the many obstacles blocking their way, and they push through when they're tired but still have miles to go. Surround yourself with salmon people. In fact, be the salmon.

Expand your purpose to include helping others. It's definitely Hard-Easy to serve others as you're trying to accomplish and juggle everything else—which is exactly why you need to make it part of your life.

When we look beyond ourselves to see and act on the needs of others, it alleviates self-absorption and anxiety. Several studies have found that giving your time and money to others will make you deeply happy, even more happy than if you spent it on yourself.

- The little decisions are actually the big decisions.

- Purpose gives life meaning and direction and fosters hope for the future.

- Be, and swim with, the Salmon People.

- Performing acts of kindness helps you live a more satisfying, engaging life.

- Find your purpose, develop your plan, and maintain your vision.

PAUSE AND THINK

- Who are the Salmon People in your life? Name them here.

_____

_____

_____

_____

_____

_____

_____

To help you define your purpose, create some lists:

- Love list

What do you love to do? Make a list.

_____

_____

_____

_____

_____

_____

_____

_____

_____

_____

_____

_____

_____

_____

_____

_____

_____

- Easy list

What activities come easy to you? Write them down. Do any of them overlap with your love list?

_____

_____

_____

_____

_____

_____

_____

_____

_____

_____

_____

_____

_____

_____

_____

_____

_____

_____

_____

- Reflection list

When have you been the happiest and most fulfilled? Write that down. After you've completed your list, revisit it. For each entry on the list, write down what specifically about each event or era made you happy.

_____

_____

_____

_____

_____

_____

_____

_____

_____

_____

_____

_____

_____

_____

_____

_____

_____

_____

_____

- Perfect-world list

This is a fun one. Complete these sentences:

  In my perfect world, I will be doing . . .

_____

_____

_____

  In my perfect world, I will be achieving . . .

_____

_____

_____

  In my perfect world, I will be the kind of person who is . . .

_____

_____

_____

  In my perfect world, I will have . . .

_____

_____

_____

_____

*In my perfect world, I will affect others'
lives by . . .*

_____

_____

_____

_____

- Who can you share your lists with?
  Come up with the names of two or three
  people who will help hold you
  accountable. Then share your lists and
  get feedback.

_____

_____

_____

_____

- What is the big goal you have in mind
  right now?

_____

_____

_____

_____

_____

- What purpose will keep you working toward that goal? What is the reason you want to achieve it?

_____

_____

_____

_____

_____

_____

_____

_____

_____

_____

_____

_____

- **From there, create a plan—not a perfect plan! Keep it simple and create momentum. Forget the massive, earth-shaking, jumbo decisions. You're going to fill out your plan with the little stuff. The most important part of the process is to keep your purpose or goal at the forefront.**

- Which way do your service scales tip—
toward selfishness or selflessness? How
can you bring them into better balance?
(Or keep them in balance?) Brainstorm
your thoughts here.

_____

_____

_____

_____

_____

_____

_____

_____

_____

_____

_____

_____

_____

_____

TAKEAWAY

The easy phase of your Hard-Easy plan—the end
result—should be so clear in your mind that the
hard parts simply fall into place. The small decisions you plan every day will build toward it. Be

the salmon person who pushes upstream with a vision of the glorious end of the journey, where the waters are rich, the current gentle, and the company delightful.

16 INVEST IN VALUE

A DEEPER LOOK AT TIME, ASSETS, AND THE PARABLE OF THE BANKER AND THE FISHERMAN

Time is the unwavering, constant variable we can use to either reach or undermine our goals. Learning to recognize when we're using time to our best advantage will increase our ability to reach our goals.

PRINCIPLE

Time is your most precious resource, your gift each morning. How you spend it will determine the trajectory of your life.

CHAPTER RECAP

Unlike any other resource in the world, time is distributed to all in equal amounts. Are we really investing our time in the assets we value most? And when it comes to ranking our assets, are we ranking them correctly?

What's an asset?

For me, an asset is anything that enriches me—that adds value to my life.

It's kind of easy to know you're wasting time when the activity actually looks like wasting time. But what about those activities that masquerade as productivity? Simply avoiding gratification is not enough. We need to spot the self-indulgence that's disguised as more virtuous activities.

Remember the parable of the fisherman and the banker from chapter 16?

Like the fisherman, we should be fixated on the why. It is the modest, simple things that bring true joy.

While we must provide for our basic needs, money is crucial only until you hit a critical mass. Research shows that once your income is enough to securely meet your basic needs, having more and more money won't increase your joy.[1]

Hard-Easy isn't just about material success. It's about making the Hard-Easy decision to invest the limited time we have in those assets we value most, on a daily basis.

- Wasting time = any activity that will not

add value to your life two, five, or ten years down the road.

- One of the biggest ways to waste time is by doing seemingly productive work that's not productive at all.

- Hard-Easy is not just about earning money and gaining wealth.

- Time is your gift each morning; how you spend it will determine the trajectory of your life.

PAUSE AND THINK

- Review how you spent your time over the last two or three days. How have you spent time well (adds value in coming years)? How can you improve your time investments?

_____

_____

_____

_____

_____

_____

_____

_____

_____

_____

_____

_____

_____

_____

_____

_____

_____

_____

_____

- Plan for how you will invest your time
  over the next two days.

_____

_____

_____

_____

_____

_____

_____

_____

TAKEAWAY

Remember, time is your most precious resource. If you're going to live Hard-Easy, you may as well live Hardest-Easiest. In other words, it can be hard to make the wisest decisions, to invest time in the things of most value, when so many other things are crying for your time. But when you spend time on the things that have the most value, you will experience the biggest returns down the road.

17 THE DECISION TO JUMP IS MADE ON THE GROUND

OR WHAT I LEARNED WHILE PLUMMETING 14,000 FEET TO THE EARTH

P lans are important, but have you ever stopped to think about why plans work on a psychological level? It's all about making the hard decisions early and from a place of safety rather than waiting until the pressure is on. This concept became concrete to me when I decided to voluntarily hurl myself from a flying plane.

PRINCIPLE

You radically increase the probability of success when you commit—truly commit—before you are placed in the heat of battle. If you haven't decided on the ground, you won't jump once you're up in the plane.

CHAPTER RECAP

The decision to jump is made on the ground, NOT on the plane. During our eight hours of skydiving training, our instructors drilled this concept into our brains. I now know why.

Even with their anxiety-quelling tactics, at about ten thousand feet, my heart was pounding so fast I felt like a hummingbird on crack. There was no part of me that wanted to leap out of that plane. This experience taught me four Hard-Easy lessons:

1. We all fear the unknown. Commit to acting in spite of fear. For many, when it's time to step out of the plane, they're not mentally prepared to leave their comfort zone. To realize the life of your dreams, you have to be as committed to saving your dreams as you are to saving your loved ones in a burning car.

2. If you want to create and have a fascinating life, you must get comfortable with being uncomfortable.

3. Willpower, grit, and self-control have a shelf life. Make your decision and carve it in stone early. You don't decide when you're at the threshold of the plane at fourteen thousand feet.

4. Plan for duress. It takes a lot of willpower and courage to fight, and we're more likely to reach that courage and willpower if we've considered and made the decision well in advance.

- To live an extraordinary life, you must be focused on and committed to taking consistent action despite misgivings and fears of the unknown.

- Living the Hard of Hard-Easy and having faith that Easy will follow can be scary; successful people feel the fear but forge ahead anyway.

- To live Hard-Easy, you need to be comfortable with being uncomfortable.

- Willpower, grit, and self-control have a shelf life.

- Decide long before you have to act.

PAUSE AND THINK

- What fears do you have associated with your dreams? Don't stop at generalizations like failure. Get specific. (You might just wish I'd assigned you to go skydiving instead.)

- Isolate one hard decision you will likely be called upon to make in your lifetime but which you've avoided. Do what you need to make that decision now. (Want to jump out of that plane yet? Chances are you're facing something far more terrifying. Keep at it.)

_____

_____

_____

_____

TAKEAWAY

Everyone I know experiences fear. What separates successful people from those who fail is their willingness to act despite the fear. The best way to deal with fear is to run headlong into it, screaming, "Bring it, Hard!" It took some courage to take that first step out of that plane. But guess what? What you are afraid of is never as bad, ugly, and ominous as you imagine it to be. In truth, taking that fourteen-thousand-foot step was one of the most liberating things I have ever done.

18 GOAL SETTING FOR THOSE WHO THINK THEY KNOW HOW TO SET GOALS

THE FIVE PRINCIPLES OF BIG-PICTURE GOALS

There are quite possibly a billion books, podcasts, apps, speeches, and media about setting goals, and yet I am amazed at how many people not only underestimate the power of goals but fail to create them properly. You've had a big-picture goal in mind as you've read through this book. I want you to examine this goal to ensure it is framed and approached in a way that offers you the most support on your Hard-Easy journey.

PRINCIPLE

Over time, simple acts can lead to greatness. When done right, goal setting can direct and motivate you to take effective, consistent action to become the person you want to become.

CHAPTER RECAP

These five principles have worked for me over and over again as I've set my mind to accomplish hard things. They're simple. They're powerful. They work. And they will work for you, too.

1. Your goal must excite you.
Make sure your goal is important to you and that you're not doing it to please someone else.

2. **Make it a SMART goal:**

Specific

- Goals must be clear and definable.

Measurable

- If you cannot measure it, you cannot manage it. If you cannot manage it, you cannot improve it. If you can't improve it, you won't achieve it.

Achievable

- If your goal is so audacious there is no

chance of realizing it, you will quickly give up on it.

Relevant

- Relevance is your why.

Timetable

- Deadlines move us.

3. Write your goals and post them.
What your mind sees, it believes. When you write your goal, use the word "will" as opposed to "would like to."

4. Develop a plan of action.
By writing down specific actions and crossing them each off as you complete them, you'll see that you're making progress. This is essential when your goal is big, audacious, stretchable, and long-term.

5. Endure.
Recognize that part of goal setting is the ongoing necessity of recalibrating and fine-tuning. Enduring to the end requires diligence, vision, determination, and flexibility.

PAUSE AND THINK

- You've kept a big goal in mind while reading this book. Take a closer look at it now.

  * Does it excite you?

  * Is it SMART?

Once you have a goal that is exciting and SMART:

- Write it down and post it where you will see it often. Don't forget to use "I will."

_____

_____

_____

_____

_____

_____

_____

_____

_____

_____

- Also, write down why the goal is important to you. How would you convey its meaning to someone else? Refine your answer until you're satisfied with it.

- Make a plan of action—a series of smaller SMART goals that will keep you on track.

_____

_____

_____

_____

_____

_____

_____

_____

_____

_____

_____

_____

_____

_____

_____

_____

_____

_____

_____

_____

TAKEAWAY

When I joined the wrestling team in eight grade, my overarching, big-picture goal gave me the strength to endure years of hard work. My goal propelled me forward—through dark times and setbacks, through times when I was ready to quit, through times when it seemed like it was all pointless. It gave me the strength to endure.

19 THE FIVE FRIENDS YOU NEED AND THE FIVE FRIENDS YOU NEED TO AVOID

In this chapter, I'm going to tell you about ten friends—the five you need to help you live Hard-Easy and the five you need to avoid so they don't hinder your Hard-Easy efforts.

PRINCIPLE

If you want to live a long, happy life, you must have a diverse, balanced, flesh-and-blood entourage that has your back through the highs and lows.

CHAPTER RECAP

Many studies over the past several decades have stressed the importance of a strong social network of friends as a critical factor of good health and happiness. True friends should make you feel revitalized and uplifted.

- **The five types of friends you need in your life are the clairvoyant, the clown, the cheerleader, the cohort, and the chaperone (the five Cs).**

The clairvoyant elevates our thinking by quietly reminding us of the consequences of our actions. The clown convinces us not to take things so seriously and to laugh at our shortcomings. The cheerleader encourages us no matter what. And the cohort is there to lean on at work when we need to vent and hang out. The chaperone listens and helps us translate the advice of the other four. They help us chart our course past apprehension and confusion.

- **There are five friends you should be wary of: the drainer, the dishonest, the dramatic, the disloyal, and the dupe (the five Ds).**

The know-it-all drainer puts down our ideas and makes us feel like crap. If the drainer is a vampire, then the dishonest is a locust, consuming our money, time, patience, and sanity. The dramatic craves attention, stirs up chaos, and always needs reassurance. Competitive and jealous, the disloyal spreads rumors, disregards our wants, and tries to look good at our expense. And the dupe pretends to make us a priority in their life, all the while flaking out on our time and interests.

- **Be wise in assessing friends who are really wolves in sheep's clothing— because they may not really be your friends at all.**

Although I have described extremes, there are friends, family members, and acquaintances who lie somewhere in between. Don't sever relationships with anyone in the hopes of making new friends you believe are better, but pay attention to those who will encourage you in your Hard-Easy decisions and those who will undermine your efforts.

PAUSE AND THINK

- See if you can identify the C friends and D friends in your life.

_____

_____

_____

_____

_____

_____

_____

_____

_____

_____

- Complete the following friend assessment to determine where you stand with your friends:

1. Am I at ease to simply be myself around my friends?

_____

_____

_____

_____

2. Of all my friends, which ones do I value most and why?

_____

_____

_____

_____

_____

3. Who is my clairvoyant, constantly encouraging me to do better?

_____

_____

4. Who is my clown, helping me not to take things so seriously?

_____

_____

5. Who is my cheerleader, always pumping me up and telling me I am great and can do this?

_____

_____

6. Who is my cohort, who has my back at work and eases the stress of my professional grind?

_____

_____

7. Who is my chaperone, translating and interpreting other friends' advice and guiding me toward my ultimate goal?

_____

_____

8. What roles do I play in my friends' lives?

_____

_____

_____

_____

9. Have I ever been a D friend?

_____

_____

_____

_____

10. How can I be a better C friend?

_____

_____

_____

_____

_____

_____

_____

_____

_____

_____

_____

_____

_____

TAKEAWAY

Over the years, I have learned that the only way to have a trusted friend is to be a trusted friend. You choose your path in life and those you want to experience it with. This world has far too much cynicism and judgment. The friends you keep close to you should provide you a safe harbor from those storms of negativity. True friends are extremely invested in you—and let you know it! The cool thing about a real friend is that their happiness is yours, and yours theirs.

20 RELATIONSHIPS

It's fairly easy to draw a link to Hard-Easy when numbers and facts are involved. It's trickier when your heart is involved. Or is it? Think about the relationship you're currently in or the relationship you dream of having. How does the law of Hard-Easy apply to finding that relationship and keeping it strong?

PRINCIPLE

Strong, long-term relationships require hard work—all the time. When you do the small, hard things regularly, Easy comes as a feeling of safety, togetherness, and peace.

CHAPTER RECAP

When it comes to finding a partner, Easy would have you focus primarily on physical appearance and the high of infatuation; you want love to be easy to form and easy to maintain. But that's the fallacy of Easy-Hard.

Beauty ebbs and flows. To find the kind of love that will carry you through the ups and downs, choose someone who shares your core values. This is so important I suggest you make a list. Keep your list to three to four things (a favorite movie or tv show doesn't count). If you struggle to identify your core values, you need to be alone with yourself and sort that out *before* seeking a relationship.

Fueling a healthy relationship requires millions of microdecisions and small gestures—daily. It's the flywheel again. Long-lasting relationships aren't made of perfect people. They are made of people who communicate, compromise, forgive, and offer understanding—people who create an environment where unconditional love can grow and thrive.

When struggles arise, and they will, communicate. Focus on the problem, not the person. Remember, empathy and anger cannot coexist. Proactively carve out time to be together. Laugh.

Set goals together, share new adventures, and while you are with your partner, dedicate your attention to them and them alone.

Above all else, there must be love. Unconditional love.

If you don't love your partner unconditionally, what the hell is it all about?

- Early love is an addiction. Get through it before you make any big decisions.

- Go into a relationship with your eyes wide open.

- Hard-Easy can help keep your relationship thriving in both an emotional and a practical sense.

PAUSE AND THINK

- Can you envision a life without them? Do you like that vision? Why or why not?

_____

_____

_____

_____

_____

_____

_____

_____

_____

_____

_____

_____

_____

_____

_____

- If you're dating, think about the qualities you want in a partner. Make a list.

_____

_____

_____

_____

_____

_____

_____

_____

_____

- Make a list of non-negotiable qualities as well as deal breakers. Go beyond physical qualities—what do you want out of a relationship?

* For further reading in this area, Develop Good Habits published the article, "24 Best Relationship Books Every Couple Should Read Together."[1]

_____

_____

_____

_____

_____

_____

_____

_____

_____

_____

_____

_____

_____

_____

- If you're in a committed relationship, pay attention to the choices you make over the course of two or three days. How often are you choosing Hard?

_____

_____

_____

_____

_____

_____

_____

_____

_____

_____

_____

_____

TAKEAWAY

Deep love takes time to grow roots and to manifest itself. We must get past the infatuation stage, take a step back, and figure out what this relationship is really all about. It's hard to do but necessary if we want to find someone we can spend the rest of our life with. Loving someone means learning to trust that person, little by little. Loving someone is seeing the good despite the bad. Loving someone is hard work.

21 THE TEN COMMANDMENTS FOR ACHIEVING ACADEMIC SUCCESS FOR THOSE WITH (OR WITHOUT) DYSLEXIA

HARD-EASY LESSONS FOR ACADEMICS

Long before I met Gordon the cowboy and heard his simple explanation of the law of Hard-Easy, I was living it. Struggling with dyslexia from elementary school on, I was tempted to take the Easy-Hard way out of pursuing higher education because of my disability. Thankfully, I applied some Hard-Easy concepts before I knew what to call them.

PRINCIPLE

You may have been born with natural talent, or you may have been born with limitations and challenges.

Either way, you must dig deep and choose Hard to achieve your goals.

CHAPTER RECAP

At some point in my youth, I started allowing my dyslexia to define me. I would tell myself that I did not need to get a college degree, let alone a higher degree. Could I even be a decent college student?

The clairvoyant wisdom of my father let me know I could defeat these velociraptors of doubt if only I fought fiercely enough—"Bring it, Hard!" The battle wouldn't be easy, but neither was it impossible to win.

Fortunately, I had other role models as well. My friend Stan helped me realize that I could use my strengths—endurance, relentlessness, people skills, creativity, persuasive speaking, and my perfectionist nature—to overcome my academic weaknesses.

The education system wanted me to read and learn like their typical student, and that was how they measured, saw, and scored me. Once I realized I did not have to play the game their way, I was off to the races.

Most, if not all, of these ten commandments can help any student earn high marks in their college courses—no dyslexia required.

Art's Scholastic Ten Commandments

1. Never miss class.

2. Sit in the second row, just off the center, away from the door.

3. Keep lecture notes, skipping every three lines on the paper to add notes later.

4. Digitally record every lecture, if possible.

5. Listen to each lecture within twenty-four hours, filling in note details (on the three lines left open).

6. Stay one day ahead of the scheduled homework.

7. Organize study groups with other students—serious students.

8. Two to three weeks into the semester, personally meet the professor.

   a. Ask for elaboration on the last lecture.

  b. Clarify the conditions needed for
    an A in the class.

  c. Ask about the A+.

9. Revisit the professor, discussing his/her background, grad school, publications, and more.

10. Network with your professors, assistant professors, tutors, and classmates.

Key Concepts

- Defy negative labels.

- Dream big.

- Use your strengths to overcome your weaknesses.

PAUSE AND THINK

- What labels have people or institutions affixed upon you?

_____

_____

_____

_____

_____

_____

- What have you or could you achieve despite those labels? Think about it.

_____

_____

_____

_____

_____

_____

_____

_____

_____

_____

_____

_____

- Have you ever used your strengths to overcome one of your weaknesses? Give an example.

_____

_____

_____

_____

_____

_____

_____

_____

_____

_____

_____

_____

_____

_____

_____

TAKEAWAY

The pursuit of perfection and excellence is spurred on by looking in the mirror every day and asking, "Can I do more?" and then doing more. We should all develop this habit and push for perfection. At the same time, we must be content with progress and understand that perfection is unachievable. We should be continually striving, pushing, learning, practicing, failing, and trying again and again. It refines us and makes us better.

22 DEATH

It was Leonardo da Vinci who said, "While I thought I was learning how to live, I have been learning how to die."

What does death have to do with the law of Hard-Easy? Anything?

PRINCIPLE

No matter who we are—Yorick or Alexander the Great —nothing can save us from the grave.

You have now.

That knowledge should be used to live every second with joy. Those who live Hard-Easy go to their deaths with a peace born of having lived a full, rich, joyful life.

CHAPTER RECAP

Logically, we all realize that death is an inescapable reality. Yet most people I know do not deeply contemplate their own mortality.

I get it.

Death is never a pleasant subject, but it is necessary to confront and reconcile our feelings of discomfort regarding it.

Even if death is the end of all ends, each human being who exists on this planet leaves a legacy. Each life touches others, and that ripple effect exists even if those affected are never aware of the influence of others' lives on their own.

Steve Jobs said, "Remembering that you are going to die is the best way I know to avoid the trap of thinking you have something to lose. You are already naked. There is no reason not to follow your heart."[1]

Do the Hard thing. Embrace the discomfort, and you'll find you feel more reconciled with the reality of death. Those who live Easy up front to avoid the later Hard die many slow, painful deaths throughout their lives. Those who live Hard-Easy experience death only once.

- The awareness of death heightens our focus on what we have today.

- If you use this awareness as a motivator, as Steve Jobs advocates, it's as if the friends and family who have passed on are motivating you from beyond.

PAUSE AND THINK

- Take a few short minutes out of your busy, frenetic schedule and call that person you are thinking of and just say, "I love you," "I need you," "I appreciate you," or "I'm sorry if I ever offended you or caused you pain." Seriously. Stop reading. Go do it now.

- Do that again tomorrow. Schedule it in your planner or set a reminder in your phone. Follow up with yourself in a week or a month: how many times did you follow through instead of hitting snooze on your alarm?

- Do it again the next day. Make it a habit.

TAKEAWAY

The law of Hard-Easy is how you take advantage of the now so that when death calls for you, you won't cower before it but face the calm known only by those who have prepared their whole lives for the next phase of their journey. We can all be great. We all have that capacity, but it takes a lot of courage, grit, and many small, consistent, hard choices to achieve it.

Life here is short. So do you with passion.

CONCLUSION
THE ULTIMATE GOAL

Now that you know the law of Hard-Easy, you are better equipped to magnify it in your life so it can bless you, not punish you.

My biggest wish is for you to become your future self and to love that person. I want you to appreciate how past you made hard choices, delayed gratification, and faced down the unknown to make your dreams come true. When it comes time to face the end and whatever is next, I wish for you to meet it with no regrets. Your family will share that peace with you.

Embrace the changes that need to be made. Race toward them. Shout those words: "Bring it, Hard!"

Today can be the day future you looks back and

says, "That was the fork in the road that led me to this wonderful life."

Make each moment a gift to future you—and when you meet that person, it will be in an extraordinary life built upon trillions of Hard-Easy decisions that put the law to work for you, not against you.

This moment is yours—spend it wisely.

MAKING A PLAN

If you're ready to put everything together, you can use these pages to write down your first goal. You know, that thing in the back of your mind since you picked up this book that has been urging you to make a change and yell, "Bring it, Hard!"

My first big-picture goal for living the law of Hard-Easy is . . .

_____

_____

_____

_____

_____

_____

_____

- I chose this goal because . . .

_____
_____
_____
_____
_____
_____
_____
_____
_____
_____
_____
_____

- I will know I have reached my goal when . . .

_____
_____
_____
_____
_____
_____
_____

• My deadline to reach this goal is . . .

_____

_____

_____

_____

• What consistent action will help me
  reach this goal?

_____

_____

_____

_____

_____

_____

_____

_____

_____

_____

_____

_____

_____

Ask yourself, is my goal SMART: **S**pecific,
Measurable, **A**chievable, **R**elevant, and fits in a
Timetable? (See chapter 18.)

Remember, choosing Hard-Easy is an accumulation of small decisions over time. Decide what you'll do today and the next to make it happen.

My first micro goal to support my big-picture goal is . . .

_____

_____

_____

_____

_____

_____

_____

- I will know I have reached my goal when . . .

_____

_____

_____

_____

_____

_____

_____

_____

_____

• My deadline to reach this goal is . . .

_____

_____

_____

_____

• What consistent action will help me reach this goal?

_____

_____

_____

_____

_____

_____

_____

_____

_____

_____

_____

_____

_____

_____

My second micro goal to support my big-picture goal is . . .

_____

_____

_____

_____

_____

_____

_____

- I will know I have reached my goal when . . .

_____

_____

_____

_____

_____

_____

_____

_____

_____

_____

_____

_____

- My deadline to reach this goal is . . .

_____

_____

_____

_____

_____

_____

- What consistent action will help me reach this goal?

_____

_____

_____

_____

_____

_____

_____

_____

_____

_____

_____

My third micro goal to support my big-picture goal is . . .

_____

_____

_____

_____

_____

_____

_____

- I will know I have reached my goal when
  . . .

_____

_____

_____

_____

_____

_____

_____

_____

_____

_____

_____

_____

_____

- My deadline to reach this goal is . . .

_____

_____

_____

_____

- What consistent action will help me reach this goal?

_____

_____

_____

_____

_____

_____

_____

_____

_____

_____

_____

_____

_____

NOTE TO THE READER

Thank you so much for taking the time to work through Hard-Easy. I hope this workbook resonates with you and inspires you to pay close attention to your choices and the consequences that will follow. I want you to know that I, too, am still learning this concept. I mutter "Bring it, Hard!" under my breath daily. If you've found even a small part of this workbook beneficial to you, it would mean a great deal if you could leave me a review on Amazon and Goodreads—and, of course, spread the word!

With sincere appreciation,
   Art

Find me at www.ArtCoombs.com

facebook.com/www.ArtCoombs.com
twitter.com/arthurfcoombs
instagram.com/arthurfcoombs
linkedin.com/in/artcoombs

NOTES

9. IN PRAISE OF GRITS

1. Angela Duckworth (blog), accessed August 13, 2019, https://angeladuckworth.com/qa/.
2. *Man's Search for Meaning* (New York: Simon & Schuster, 1984), 81.

12. SILENCING THE TOXIC WHISPERS OF SHAME

1. Brené Brown, "Shame vs. Guilt," Brené Brown (website), January 14, 2013, https://brenebrown.com/articles/2013/01/14/shame-v-guilt/.

14. GARLIC AGAINST THE INSTANT-GRATIFICATION VAMPIRE

1. Kevin McSpadden, "You Now Have a Shorter Attention Span Than a Gold-fish," Time, May 14, 2015, http://time.com/3858309/attention-spans-goldfish/.
2. Sofie Bates, "A Decade of Data Reveals That Heavy Multi-taskers Have Reduced Memory, Stanford Psychologist Says," Stanford News, October 25, 2018, https://news.stanford.edu/2018/10/25/decade-data-reveals-heavy-multitaskers-reduced-memory-psychologist-says/.
3. Kendra Cherry, "How Multitasking Affects Productivity and Brain Health," Verywell Mind, updated March 16, 2019, https://www.verywellmind.com/multitasking-2795003.

16. INVEST IN VALUE

1. Daniel Kahneman and Angus Deaton, "High Income Improves Evaluation of Life but Not Emotional Well-Being," PNAS, September 7, 2010, https://www.pnas.org/content/early/2010/08/27/1011492107.

20. RELATIONSHIPS

1. "24 Best Relationship Books Every Couple Should Read Together," Develop Good Habits, September 30, 2019, https://www.developgoodhabits.com/best-relationship-books/.

22. DEATH

1. Maria Forbes, "Steve Jobs: 'Death Is Very Likely the Single Best Invention of Life,'" Forbes, October 5, 2011, https://www.forbes.com/sites/moiraforbes/2011/10/05/steve-jobs-death-is-very-likely-the-single-best-invention-of-life/#a58454329b06.

ABOUT THE AUTHOR

Best-selling author, dynamic speaker, and leadership guru Arthur F. Coombs III brings decades of global expertise to readers, audiences, and corporations through his visionary and innovative practices.

Founder and CEO of KomBea Corporation, Art has served for about twenty years developing and marketing tools that blend human intelligence and automation. Art's best-selling book, *Don't Just Manage—Lead!,* has been hailed by some of the nation's top executives. His second best-selling book,

Human Connection: How the "L" Do We Do That?, provides a powerful formula for deep and meaningful connections with others. His third book, *Hard Easy: A Get-Real Guide for Getting the Life You Want* inspired him to create this corresponding workbook so that people can put the lessons in the book into practical use, working through intellectual exercises to create the life they want.

Before founding KomBea, Art served as EVP of Strategic Initiatives for FirstSource. As CEO and founder of Echopass Corporation, he helped build the world's premier contact-center hosting environment. Art has served as Sento Corporation's CEO, managing director, and vice president of Europe for Sykes Enterprises, and has worked for organizations such as Hewlett-Packard, VLSI Research, and RasterOps.

Art's vast experience with people and organizations has led him to share transformative principles for creating a fantastic life—principles you can now access within these pages.

facebook.com/ArthurFCoombs
twitter.com/ArthurFCoombs
instagram.com/arthurfcoombs
linkedin.com/in/artcoombs

ALSO BY
ARTHUR F. COOMBS III

Hard Easy: A Get Real Guide for Getting the Life You Want

In this dynamic self-help book, Art Coombs challenges you to take up the mantle of Hard Easy. From remarkable stories to real-life examples, he demonstrates why it's better to put in effort now and reap the rewards later.

Get your copy at your favorite retailer.

Don't Just Manage—Lead!

Using the tools, dynamic analogies, and examples laid out in Arthur F. Coombs III's *Don't Just Manage—Lead!*, you'll learn how to identify and apply the traits of a leader to your life.

Get your copy at your favorite retailer.

Human Connection: How the "L" Do We Do That?

In his book *Human Connection: How the "L" Do We Do That?*, Arthur F. Coombs III offers easy tools and memorable analogies to help you do just that. By taking you through five simple "Ls", he'll teach you to navigate a busy, techno-centric world.

Get your copy at your favorite retailer.